Mary Ford Neal

Dawning

Indigo Dreams Publishing

First Edition: Dawning
First published in Great Britain in 2021 by:
Indigo Dreams Publishing
24, Forest Houses
Cookworthy Moor
Halwill
Beaworthy
Devon
EX21 5UU

www.indigodreams.co.uk

Mary Ford Neal has asserted her right under the Copyright, Designs and Patents Act 1988 to be identified as the author of this work.
© Mary Ford Neal 2021

ISBN 978-1-912876-52-5

British Library Cataloguing in Publication Data. A CIP record for this book can be obtained from the British Library.

Designed and typeset in Palatino Linotype by Indigo Dreams.
Cover design by Ronnie Goodyer at Indigo Dreams
Printed and bound in Great Britain by 4edge Ltd.

Papers used by Indigo Dreams are recyclable products made from wood grown in sustainable forests following the guidance of the Forest Stewardship Council.

For Tom

Acknowledgements

I owe thanks to my parents, my brother, and my husband, who have all been sources of great strength and support during the period of writing this book. In particular, I thank my dad, who taught me poetry at school and fostered my love of it.

Heartfelt thanks are due to GB Clarkson and Zannah Kearns for the generosity with which they have read my work and allowed me to call on their advice; their friendship and wisdom are indispensable to me. I also thank the many friends and colleagues (on and offline) who have been my early readers and encouragers.

Profound thanks to Dawn Bauling and Ronnie Goodyer at Indigo Dreams Publishing for their support and expert guidance, and for making my first collection a reality.

I am grateful to the editors of the journals where some of the poems in this collection were first published: 'Street magic', 'What I like', 'My husband is losing his shit', 'Ebbing (Part I)', 'Ebbing (Part II)', and 'in which i wish god on you' were all first published in *Dodging the Rain;* 'Dawning' and 'Coffee' were first published in *One Hand Clapping*; 'Gestation' was first published in *IceFloe Press*; 'The sea-wife' was first published in *Janus Literary*; 'The hunger moon draws out the wolves' was first published in *Crow & Cross Keys*; 'stars inside' was first published in *The Mark Literary Review*; and 'as if we never were' was first published in *FEED*.

Above all, I thank my young son, Tom, who has been the loudest and most enthusiastic supporter of my writing. This book is dedicated to him, with all my love.

Dawning is Mary Ford Neal's debut poetry collection.

CONTENTS

Dawning

Mouth Villanelle

I told the world I didn't love you. Why?
        A fear of what comes after flesh and bone.
An oath, an affirmation, and a lie.

A mouth that promised once, now gaping dry.
        The night comes in and queers the telephone.
I told the world I didn't love you. Why?

The only word allowed me is Goodbye,
        but I can speak three things with that alone:
an oath, an affirmation, and a lie.

This mouth malfunctions, set to falsify;
        my other mouth's a monster I disown.
I told the world I didn't love you. Why?

Saint Apollonia sings a lullaby,
        a shattered song through shattered lips. A moan,
an oath, an affirmation, and a lie.

The rubble of my promise chokes a cry.
        Let all my mouths from all my heads be torn.
I told the world I didn't love you. Why?
        An oath, an affirmation, and a lie.

Approaching

And suddenly you're there, fifty yards away, bobbing between the heads of oblivious shoppers, moving towards me in your well-worn woollen coat, well-tucked scarf and easy gait. I'm on the spot where we said we'd meet, a vice of cold clamping my feet to the pavement. You must have spotted me, but instead of meeting my eye you stop right there, in the middle of the afternoon clamour, causing a small gap to open around you like a knot in wood. Adopting a vaguer expression than usual, you pat yourself down, pull a map from an inside breast pocket, and begin rotating it, your glance alternating between map and street. Now, craning your neck back, you gaze at the tops of buildings, as if trying to work out what kind of place this might be, which street – which city, even. By now, I'm smiling. You shuffle round on the spot, crumpled map and crumpled brow, and seeming to get your bearings a bit, start towards me again, more hesitantly than before. I'm laughing. And then the finale: there, in the middle of this street you know so well, you politely interrupt a passing stranger, a well-dressed man your own age, and have a brief conversation with him that culminates in him pointing his gloved hand straight at me. You're grinning broadly, all gratitude, touching him lightly on the overcoated elbow as he moves off, pleased with himself, your unwitting extra. I'm almost applauding now – a virtuoso performance. And now you make a great show of seeing me, raising your hand in exaggerated greeting. My face creases in laughter. Yet you saw me all along, and took your time to get here. The thought appears and is banished.

And the smile never leaves your face.

It never leaves your face.

Street magic

I don't believe in magic. But something
hovers along these streets, something
like dust not settling hangs just above
the slippery cobbles, and it's more than
the messy flash of reflected streetlight
and it's more than the colourful spill from some
long gone car, lying now in the gutter
as though someone had pierced a rainbow
and let it fall sighing down to die here
in the dark, by a drain, with the swollen fag-ends
and the dog urine and the spit of the loud lads.
This is something else – our shoes splash through it
whatever it is, and I swear it makes our stepping lighter.
My feet might fly, and any second I might be gone
unless I grab your arm to stop myself,
which I never would.

Midnight triolet
After G.B. Clarkson, 'On a Hill'

You come from madness and moonlight;
I come from candled calm, and meet you here
in shallow breath, beneath a sweep of night.
You come from madness and moonlight,
real-mythic, dead-alive, alight,
chaos of black death, breath of fear.
You come from madness and moonlight;
I come from candled calm, and meet you here.

What I like

Tell me what you like,
you say, and your murmur is summer-thick.
Tell me what you like.
Because although your chin is resting on my stomach,
and you've tasted the fresh sweat on my collarbone,
you don't know what I like.
Tell me…

Very well.

I like a tidy desk. I like to sit upstairs on the bus.
I like bland food, and I like sleeping on sofas with
the television on. I like the way my mother always
wears clothes that suit her perfectly. I liked
my grandmother's command of a room. I like it when
a favourite song begins on the radio, even though I have
the CD beside me on the car seat. I like taking a book
from the shelf after years of neglect, and seeing the bits
I've underlined, and wondering why, and finding my old
scribbled notes in the margins, especially if they're
sarcastic, or contain exclamation marks. I like
very cold weather, and wearing layers. I like myself
for surviving the early realisation that true happiness
would always elude me, and I like praying. I like people
who say what they mean, and I like the last third
of a candle. I like sparrows, and clearing my plate.
I like having a notebook nearby at all times. I like
spending whole days without speaking, and I like
descending bass scales.

I like being helpful.
I hope this is helpful.

Terminal

A miracle I'm here at all; my autopilot working well.
Book flight, find taxi, navigate security,
and get me to the gate,
despite the fact I woke today in hell.

By tea-time, I'll be hugged tight to his chest, inhaling wool.
Now, I exist in half-hour bursts, in crackling,
sobbing calls, self-cursed—
a wandering terminal ghoul.

My heart and eyelids swollen shut against the unexpected pain.
My throat bricked up, my face crisscrossed with horror,
but all is not lost—
I have the last seat on the plane.

My husband is losing his shit

because apparently a woman who looks just like me
went to another city   and ended up drinking for hours
with a man whose name is such a profanity
that neither of us can say it   it would be like speaking
the name of the Devil   and what she did next with this man
was also unspeakable   and *she looks just like me.*

Apparently she looks just like me   but her eyes glittered
she laughed like a fanfare
and her behaviour was so unlike mine
that I'm sure there could be no mistake   and I'm sure
that my husband is worrying unnecessarily   and I'm sure
that there's no need for him to be waving
someone else's arms around
and wearing someone else's face

and no need to be shelling me with deadly words
but apparently
the resemblance is uncanny   so much so that despite the fact
that I would never do those things   would never
would never
and her eyes   and she laughed   and her behaviour
but
you see
she looks
so much
like
me.

No Man's Land

They found me lying out in No Man's Land
my people
and brought me back
behind their barricades
reclaimed me piece by piece
a lock of hair   a tooth   a tiny shoe
curated me.

They found my wreckage out in No Man's Land
my people
and brought it back
in swept-up smithereens
the dust of me
and through decades they salvaged what they could
delivered me.

They wrapped me in their plaintive chords and murmurs
things I never heard in No Man's Land
where everything was foreign but familiar
vivid but untrue
and once preserved   they laid me
under glass

where gentle hands will try and fail to reach me
and gentle lips will form unheard petitions
and No Man's Land feels very far away
but I am there   escaping every day
although my body lies
in sanctuary.

Curtains

On a hard hospital bed in the city
with curtains pulled round
I knew   it was over.

And later that evening
back home
you stood at my door
wearing a weak smile

all bedside manner.

What was it? It was   nothing.
Something abdominal?
Something   abominable.
Something that was
                    not
                your
                    business.

                    I was tidied up and polished
                            but I wore black
                    and you brought me lilies
                        which you placed into
                            my empty arms
                            while I looked
                        over your shoulder.

Dawning

They stir, begin to gather up their clothes.
Morning leaks in where curtains fail to meet.
He leaves, releasing monsters as he goes.

Funny how, soon as feeble daylight shows,
the bold, metallic night admits defeat.
They stir, begin to gather up their clothes.

Unwelcome sounds and smells of day impose
themselves; flashes of last night can't compete.
He leaves, releasing monsters as he goes.

Nothing was quite the way she had supposed
it would be. She takes cover in the sheet.
He stirs, begins to gather up his clothes.

A quick kiss, and her recognition grows:
she should regard the matter as complete.
He leaves, releasing monsters as he goes.

As of this moment, the sum of what she knows
is the soft click of the door as he retreats.
She stirs, begins to gather up her clothes.
He leaves, releasing monsters as he goes.

Breakneck

Unrolling all around me, bare country seized
by winter, frosted and forsaken, a memory
of green interred in crusted cold.

From far away, a scarlet shriek obliterates
the peace, ancient and mocking, flung
from the hellish throat of a devil-black crow.

An ugly music, heavy with the absence
of all that is holy, and a hint of amusement
that almost stops my heart.

Like a rumble of unseasonal thunder
we crack for home, through frigid air
that still vibrates with menace.

The riding is fast in midwinter,
breakneck it is, and my bird's feet
near frozen to me, and me to my horse.

you are like water

that rushes to the surface, and breaks it,
and is fated from that moment to begin
running, getting ever farther from its source,
picking up speed as it goes. there's no returning.
fast-flowing water is clear because
it keeps moving and forgets all it touches;
and so with you. and as for me, i am unclear,
and cannot forgive you for being
like water, as i always knew you were.

Ophelia

It's lovely lying here, my love,
in the dim cool, where all I see shimmers
and streams wander over my face
on their way to the pool.

The streams bring small fish by, my love,
whose filmy fins smooth out my brow gently,
and the constant washing
cleans off my sins.

As long as I am lying here, my love,
I live and feel. Compared with this,
a soily, wormy grave
could not appeal.

If I am salvaged from this place, my love,
and made to lie where I can see no shimmer
and feel no kindly fins,
I worry I may die.

Ebbing (Part I)

Here on the lengthening shore I watch
as the tide laps away predictably
the tide that submerged me so recently
that its film still clings to my skin
and draws a shudder.

If I depended only on my senses
I'd be unsure, the inching away so slight
it could easily be mistaken
but I rely instead on what I know
of tides, and how they leave.

I also know that tides return
so by then I'll have raised myself
from my damp seat, and studded
with imprints of shell and stone
I'll have wandered back to dry, dry land
where laws of nature promise tides don't follow.

Ebbing (Part II)

So I resuscitate myself, smooth out the creases and I stand
a moment, face to the curdled sky and then begin
the dreamlike journey back to dry, dry land.
But these are sea legs now, and might rebel,

and yes, I feel dragged backwards out to sea.
My lips are silent now and cannot move, but if they could
how would they keep from whispering *scuttle me?*
I know I cannot promise that they would.

I know the sea is full of little deaths, and I'm afraid
of riptides, and of pounding rains and winds.
I know that I will spend my life on dry, dry land
sorry for these and all my other sins.

Disillusion

What looks like magic
   is really disappointment.
      Cross-legged in front of the TV, I wore
         the adults down, and they admitted
            that no-one could really do those things.
         Although they encouraged me
      to admire the cleverness, I resented it
     and have resented cleverness ever since
   as trickery, a poor substitute for something else.
And now I watch as you wave your hands
   and make things happen.
     A girl appears.
       A meal appears.
         A taxi appears.
         A girl is cut in half.
       A girl disappears.
     And I think you might be magic,
   but really, all it means is that
I can't believe in you.

Inventory

A voice speaks behind me, but I can't turn.
I've already left for the land of my birth,
my head-down scurried streets,
my purple earth, my plunging hills that seem
to smoke when the sky is low,
my fractured place, all faults, a lacework
of injury held together by a godforsaken beauty
that takes all breath equally, that cannot be denied,
even by those who deny for a living
and do so under oath. The beauty gets them, yes
it whispers itself to them like a rumour until
they cannot but repeat it, cannot but believe it,
cannot help but have it, they become it, they belong to it
and it to them.

The gasping beauty of my unsafe place. I have it too,
the disease for it. A plum sky, darkly churning,
drags me in to its deep drama.
A stack of stone spindles like pipes on an organ.
A precipice. A hydra.
A plate of leftovers. A lullaby. A dog without a tail.
A man who played mouth-organ
and danced in the butcher's queue,
and died in a doorway one night of cold.

By the greying out of these things I endure;
they surface only in the final drift to sleep.
I miss you greatly, and will always, but miss what?
A nothing. A wisp of thought only. A figment. A shade.

And the waves hurry to break themselves on the rocks below,
like a list of all the things I wish you were.

Coffee

He is there first, unquiet, rolling and unrolling
a paper napkin, eyes fixed on an image
on the inside of his skull.
She enters on puppet limbs, sits down too sharply,
folds herself up like a tripod, telescoping, knees jutting.
Adjusting and readjusting. Twisting away,
neck sinews writhing,
she tries to smile. Her teeth are daggers.
Thanks for coming, he says, I know you weren't sure.
Her head shakes machine-like, denying she's here.
Two black coffees, he says to the waitress. Listen, he says,
I'm so, so sorry. I'm a dickhead, he says – he's smiling.
Yes you are you are you are you are, say the neck sinews.
I'm a complete idiot, he says. Her mouth opens. O.
The sound that comes out is: *Don't worry about it*
but her eyes teem with something.
The coffees appear, and he sets about using
the heavy metal spoon to tear the smooth caramel foam
from the surface, exposing the darkness beneath.
She crosses her legs so tightly they hurt, not trying out
any of the phrases she rehearsed on the train.
Now she is here, and he is opposite, she sees
that dark, bitter observations wouldn't work,
that he'd only agree with her, smiling, and that anyway,
none of it matters. All her angles are pointing
in different directions, her face and all its features
are the colour of milk. He says, I'm glad we're cool.
He says, maybe we'll laugh about it one day.
He laughs *today*. He spreads out.
The sinews spasm.
The coffee bites her tongue.

Deciding not to see him

If prickling doubt is rising
in your chest,
don't make the trip.
It's not too late.
Even if you are
already sitting in
the driver's seat:
indicate,
pull over,
press the brake,
a three-point turn,
and head for home.
Yes, there may be
a tricky conversation
on the phone,
or, if that might
unscrew you,
just an awkward text.
A few seconds
of discomfort.
Perhaps you'll weep.
But what comes next:
a deep bath of relief,
a fire you lit yourself,
a book, or, if you lack
the focus,
just TV.
A mug of hot milk.
Sleep.

Three resurrections

Three times I've done it
three times I've cracked open hard earth
hauled myself up
activated my lungs
faked a rosy glow
and moved among the breathing
with a convincing air.

But resurrected life is fragile
threatening always to collapse
and so I need to take tremendous care
not to catch my foot in a root
a burrow
anything of the Underneath
that would suck me back down
airless.

It's safest not to move
but it's easy to grow weary of a still life
a pretty picture of living things
that might as well be dead
a life in two dimensions
flattened
diminished.

Yes – every time I've tired quickly
run for cover
got to ground just in time.
Look at me now
collapsing into earth that accepts me eagerly
and feels so much like home.

But now I know I can do it.
I can live and die at will.

It lies

It lies, it waits, it lives, it breathes
it hides, it hates, it boils, it seethes
it finds, it traps, it wraps, it wreathes.

It smiles, it nods, it waves, it greets
it flirts, it gropes, it throbs, it beats
it bites, it tears, it gnaws, it eats.

It stalks, it preys, it steals, it snares
it goads, it taunts, it haunts, it scares
it soils, it spoils, it wastes, it wears.

Gestation

After the third trimester, sickness fades;
kicking diminishes. Needing to breathe
again, in airless panic I stretch out
in bed, coaxing my organs back to life:
pleading with lungs to wake and plant a bloom
in each cheek; promising ribs it won't be long.

But hasn't it already been too long,
and still no sign of when it might be out?
More than a year I've watered, fed, and breathed
for this offspring burgeoning as I fade,
expanding as I tend it into life,
greying my letters out, blanching my bloom.

What drudgery to bring a thing to bloom!
I do begin to wonder, as I long
for air, if this could be, not a new life,
but an old master plan to catch me out,
to dim my mind and set my looks to fade,
and finally, to trick away my breath.

I notice that it pains me when I breathe.
Whenever I inhale, an inkblot blooms
behind my eyes, vivid but quick to fade.
Monstering here inside me for so long,
what is this thing I made, but can't let out;
fostered, festered, and fused to me for life?

Only my child, who did not ask for life
but has it anyway, who cannot fade,
but yet can never spring toward the bloom
of daylight, open eyes, blood, birth, and breath.
I grieve for her; her lifespan will be long
and punishing, and cruel, and wear me out.

I'm welded to her, though; can't do without
her dark matter, fierce energy, her life
force – they're the fires that sustain me along
the way, now that my own has lost its bloom.
She'll boil here quietly, under my breath,
and when she's done with me, she'll let me fade.

Could I *unfade*, remember how to breathe?
Could I break out and claim my afterlife?
Perhaps, perhaps. To bloom, though, takes so long.

A Bad Idea

Ah, God help me, I'm always breaking things.
       Said with a rueful smile.
Perhaps you should stay home today I say
Or spend some time outdoors?
Ah no he says *I'm going shopping. There's*
a great thing I saw online…
       I hold my breath
….*a tea set.*

For fuck's sake.
It's as if he can't remember what he did
the last time, and the time before,
and how he always feels when it happens.
You don't actually like tea I say
and you've had so many tea sets, and
they don't last long…
       I brace myself

…and then there's the problem of how you
go about shopping for them.
       Another rueful smile.
I study his awkward bulk.
Can he not see himself?
What does a graceless thing like him
need a tea set for?
       Don't ask me to go with you.

I remember the last time
backing into displays, the dumb look of
confusion and failure
woundedness even
his haunches banking massively in the aisles
shattering all kinds of lovely things
failing to orient himself
in civilised space.

He belongs in a field where he can
paw the ground, charge and bellow
and mount other thoughtless creatures.
But he wants a tea set for some reason,
and so he will keep inserting himself
into china shops
until finally he realises
that the whole idea is Bull.

Aubade
*For Zannah Kearns**

The little homes pool in the hollows
puddling back toward the horizon
and deep mist tucks them in making them wistful
and muffling their early morning goings-on.
It's all for me   this pigeon sky   these pastel fields
there's only me   alone here and buckling
under my headful of half-thoughts.

What lies you told
in words   in smiles   in seemings.
What lies I welcomed in
my wisdom set to silent   vibrating
in a neglected corner of myself   ignored.

But dawn unfolds now across the fields
and darkness has no answer.

I force myself to remember how   even as our faces touched
I knew you were   would always be   a stranger
my sense of recognising you a lie to myself.
In fact *I do not know you*   and it was all for nothing
for nothing
for nothing.

These things acknowledged   a depth-charge
tears up through me   surfaces as a small silence
and mingles with the vast silence outside
that spreads for miles in every direction
with the pigeon sky   with the pastel morning.

---

* *who also loves a pigeon sky.*

Fade to grey

There's a lot of dusk in this country, and
too many figures that slip in and out of sight
was it raining heavily that night?
just as you think you're going to reach them.
Yet despite all the twilight, some things shine.

Like the shock of a brick factory wall crashing
enormous and Victorian into our modern evening
did you hold my elbow when my ankle turned on a cobble?
reminding us of all the difficulty with which
we were brought to our wasted comfort.

And I remember running my hand along the rich
wood on the bar, and it felt like silk. And your words
was there an ace of spades on the nape of your neck?
were also like silk, silk nets into which I swam
and which caught me, but only once or twice.

And there was a glass on the countertop, all
decadent facets, like a thirties ballroom
isn't it funny how hollowness can feel so heavy?
which I think we both sipped from, and I imagined
pouring guests' drinks while Fred Astaire perched on the arm
of a chair.

You called for a taxi, and showed me its progress
on the screen of your phone, and what I should have done
I think the dusk is swallowing you now, godspeed
was get into that taxi alone and let a large distance open
between us, but we got in together and it opened anyway.

I cannot go to sea

When you reared up like a wave
    shaking its thousand white fists at me   I wondered
        if I'd go under quickly or if
    you planned instead to erode me.

The tide hauls litter in and out
    and seabirds overhead scream
        that they love me   and want to kill me
    and note by blaring note
I decide to let them.

A cloud crossed my soul and I felt
    your face in it   but then I remembered
        others who used to be monsters
    and are now only people   so I sent the fear back
unopened.

You know I cannot go to sea
    my element is air   and you cannot come ashore
        and so I sign to you from here.
    Water is your element   you don't need to keep
your head above it.

Report of a sinking

With solemn fervour, this boy in his captain's hat is describing to me the sinking of a particular ship. Did you know, he says, that it was caused by the fact that the ship realised it was on a collision course with another ship, and attempted to turn out of the other ship's path, and that if it had kept to its original course they'd have missed one another? No, I say, I didn't know that. And did you know, he says, that the captain of the *RMS Queen Mary* once delayed its departure for New York for six hours, waiting at Cherbourg for a Jewish family fleeing the Nazis who were held up at the French border? I did not, I say. Then he says, did you know that when he received news of the distress call from the *RMS Titanic,* the captain of the *RMS Carpathia* gave orders to switch off the ship's heating and hot water and redirect all energy to the engines so they'd reach the stricken vessel as quickly as possible? I did not know that, and nor did I know that the passengers on the sinking *SS Andrea Doria* cried when they saw the lights of the *SS Île de France,* because they knew then that their lives were saved. But did you know, he says, that a doomed ship can lie on its side on the surface for a very long time before the final plunge?

Ah yes, I say. That I did know.

The sea-wife

I tried to marry a wave.

He came so softly, twice a day, bringing me gifts,
seaglass and songs,
and his devotion to me was a wonder of the world.
And over time, through painstaking erosion,
he gently shaped my heart into a small boat.

I found a ring left lying on the sand,
and knew he meant to marry me.
But next time, he came in as weak as water,
towed by an emaciated moon,
and somehow his devotion was lethargic,
and lacked the power to lift my boat and take it.

I tried to put my arms around him, vainly,
and as he washed away I tasted saltwater;
he must have wept at being made to leave me.
And he whispered, and I caught it on the breeze,
that I should place the ring on my own finger,
and take great care to keep my heart in boat-form.

And he is out there now, swirling and crashing,
his crest festooned with broken bits of boats;
then calming, gently finding foreign beaches
that remind him of the beach where he once found me.
I know how it must pain him not to find me now,

and I sit here,
sea-wife for fifteen years.

The hunger moon draws out the wolves

From the sharpest parts of the night they appear,
wearing borrowed light.
Those that can cross water do,
those that cannot pace the bank,
howl their helplessness into the space between,
and the forests darken and fold up
oyster-like, doubling down on their treasures.

Once in hushed woods during the thick hours
I was bitten by a starving soul
who seemed sorry about catching me:
would there be a woodcutter? But
I didn't grudge him the moment of relief,
or the passing taste of my juice on his tongue;
I took the wound and pitied him, and we parted
on an understanding.

I look for him sometimes, expecting nothing:
he was a half-dead thing even then
and will have settled into earth long ago,
yet sometimes if the darkness shifts
in a certain way under a hunger moon
and in just the right wildness, I feel the soup
of my blood stir, the wound sings, and my left arm
braces for a bite.

The sharp winter sun

We collided one morning, an accident
in the sharp winter sun,
and after mild words and squinted enquiries
you noticed something flashing angrily on my finger,
and you said what you had to,
but something slipped from your eyes,
and you fumbled for tissues and words to mop it up.

Because you had cried, you said
you were just so very, very happy
and because I am kind I pretended to believe you,
and off you went, and I stood waiting to cross,
and as they turned the corner,
driver after driver had to pull down their visors
against the sharp winter sun.

And I stayed awhile, looking
at a perfect vapour trail
a pretty white scar frozen into the sky.

stars inside

my very-missed, when will you hold me again? the awayness is becoming too much. in the night, when i jolt open & find it's only an hour since i fell asleep, in those moments the bridge to morning seems too far, & too frail, & i think i see fraying on some of the ropes, & i hesitate to risk my weight on it. there are rocks below. & when will you hold me? the windows fill with ink & all the space inside me (i think it's mainly space inside now) fills with stars, & each one is a reflection of a light in your streets, a sighting of you. & a hope for you. but your streets are bright & busy, even at this hour, & do not notice my awayness, & you'll never hold me again, i know this. & how do we hope in the face of knowing? it shouldn't be possible, but i do; people do.

Voyager

I've heard people saying that they dream of galaxies,
and of the unimaginable time it would take
to travel across them, but I,
I dream only of being completely still
while the fluttering pulse of your tide comes
and goes at the edges of my dry land,
inviting me to slip my rope, fall into
the flow, and be carried for a while,
until I become caught on an interfering root. There,
pinned in foam, I'll watch as you disappear
from view, taken by the flow, and though I will sorrow
a little for my own stuckness, I will cheer
for you, Voyager.

Extra darling

Don't be sad, extra darling, as you move
toward the kerb and on into the blare
and hustle of the road. You were always going to be
too much and not enough for me.

I had more sweethearts than I could comfortably carry
and so I stopped and set you down,
not on the pitiless pavement
but on the tender verge, with daisies for company.

Don't be sad because you were surplus,
because my heart was already full
of the wrong things; just say a prayer,
look in both directions, and be brave.

I had more sweethearts than I could comfortably carry
and so I laid you down as gently as I could,
but your heart is still sweet,
and the fast lane has nothing for you to fear.

in which i wish god on you

let god be everywhere, like they say it is, let it flow like water
between all the cracks in you, like sunlight into every dark
place in you where the gloom will be powerless against the
sheer fact of it. let god be a bloodhound with your scent in its
nose, and follow you into every room, into every one of your
conversations; in every rise and fall of your chest, let god be.

and let god breathe fire, visible only to the things that mean you harm

and let god and the fire cremate every last one of them and
carry you along on the warm air cushion their burning makes,
straight down the middle away from roadside ditches and
thorns, smoothly over ruts and holes. let god flow into every
cell of you, from the roots of your hair to the tips of your toes
and saturate you, not to drown you but to baptise you, and
water you, and may you drink god.

A few questions about Love

And is Love a creature then / with perfect DNA
twisting infinitely inside it / and has it been sharpening itself
over millions of years into what it now is?
And what kind of creature would Love be anyway
would it be like a mammal / a sociable thing or would it
hatch looking nothing like itself / already alone?
And does it scent blood / and does it pick up the scent
and run with it / and is it tracked in its turn?
Is it a predator then / and not a peaceful thing
that passes its days gently? / Does it seem gentle maybe
but show you its claws when you're too close to run?
I know that Love is wild / not a domestic thing
but more than that / I don't pretend to know.

as if we never were

no photographs of us / no friends in common
no gifts / no letters pressed in books
no public words

just bits of binary / floating fragments
of loving litter / circling cyberspace
like flockless birds

and if i die / no-one will think to tell you
and if you die / no-one will let me know

a meteor could strike / the sun could flare
the poles could flip / the vacuum collapse
a bomb go off / a black hole pass too close
Doomsday could come and go / and i'd be unaware.

the blast furnace

if you can push past
the slag
the pig iron
past unendurable heat
there is stillness
at the centre of the blast furnace
stillness
in the heart of man-made hell
as village ponds are still
as august air is still
as the wings of dead birds are still
past pain
peace.

humming

not clear music, but a faint
humming, like bees hum; I suppose
wasps hum too, but we don't like that
association as much,
do we?

a slight noise that pulls at the
edges of my concentration, prevents
me from abandoning myself
fully to my book

a book I've longed to read, a
book given to me by someone I loved
when he gave it, which wasn't
terribly long ago
only last summer

yet it feels like a long life ago, and
the book is a lump of dry paper in
my hands, my hands in a prayer-like
attitude, my attitude at odds
with itself

and I'm not sure whether
the humming is outside or if
my mind is playing me bee-noise
to make me put this book away
and him with it.

To the person who left my apartment a moment ago
After Edwin Morgan, 'One Cigarette'

No dregs of you. No smouldering cigarette. No fire.
    No last cold mouthful that never knew a mouth.

Other than a slight unsteadiness, you leave me with
    no imprint, on myself or on my couch.

A piano somewhere nearby is in mourning—
    its ghost hymn wanders through the walls, bereft.

The magnets on my fridge now say: "Before we die, we live!"
    I'll live, then, knit together all that's left.

In years to come, I'll plant an ancient rabbit
    and live to see it overwhelmed by moss.

It sleeps in the hall cupboard, crackled Verdigris.
    It holds my future universe of loss.

Europa lost her fear and climbed aboard the bull
    that stole her trust with gentleness that lied.

Your pavement steps ring off and leave me knitting.
    I told the world I didn't love you. Why?

Indigo Dreams Publishing Ltd
24, Forest Houses
Cookworthy Moor
Halwill
Beaworthy
Devon
EX21 5UU
www.indigodreams.co.uk